The Peer And The Prophet: Being The Duke Of Argyll's Article On The Prophet Of San Francisco, And The Reply Of Henry George

George Douglas Campbell

THE PEER AND THE PROPHET.

BEING

THE DUKE OF ARGYLL'S

'ARTICLE ON

"THE PROPHET OF SAN FRANCISCO,"

AND THE REPLY OF

HENRY GEORGE,

ENTITLED,

"THE REDUCTION TO INIQUITY."

REPRINTED, BY PERMISSION, FROM

"THE NINETEENTH CENTURY."

LONDON:

WILLIAM REEVES, 185, FLEET STREET, E.C.

GLASGOW:

THE SCOTTISH LAND RESTORATION LEAGUE, 80, RENFIELD STREET.

THE REDUCTION TO INIQUITY.

"In this paper it has not been my aim to argue," says the Duke of Argyll, in concluding his article entitled "The Prophet of San Francisco." It is generally waste of time to reply to those who do not argue. Yet, partly because of my respect for other writings of his, and partly because of the ground to which he invites me, I take the first opportunity I have had to reply to the Duke.

In doing so, let me explain the personal incident to which he refers, and which he has seemingly misunderstood. In sending the Duke of Argyll a copy of "Progress and Poverty" I intended no impertinence, and was unconscious of any impropriety. Instead, I paid him a high compliment. For, as I stated in an accompanying note, I sent him my book, not only to mark my esteem for the author of the "Reign of Law," but because I thought him a man superior to his accidents.

I am still conscious of the profit I derived from the "Reign of Law," and can still recall the pleasure it gave me. What attracted me, however, was not, as the Duke seems to think, what he styles his "nonsense chapter." On the contrary, the notion that it is necessary to impose restrictions upon labour seems to me strangely incongruous, not only with free trade, but with the idea of the dominance and harmony of natural laws, which in preceding chapters he so well develope. Where such restrictions as Factory Acts seem needed in the interests of labour, the seeming need, to my mind, arises from previous restrictions, in the removal of which, and not in further restrictions, the true remedy is to be sought. What attracted me in the "Reign of Law" was the manner in which the Duke points out the existence of physical laws and adaptations which compel the mind that thinks upon them to the recognition of creative purpose. In this way the Duke's book was to me useful and grateful, as I doubt not it has been to many others.

My book, I thought, might, in return, be useful and grateful to the Duke—might give him something of that "immense and instinctive pleasure " of which he has spoken as arising from the recognition of the grand simplicity and unspeakable harmony of universal law. And in the domain in which I had, as I believed, done something to point out the reign of law, this pleasure is, perhaps, even more intense than in that of which he had written. For in physical laws we recognise only intelligence, and can but trust that infinite wisdom implies infinite goodness. But in social laws he who looks may recognise beneficence as well as intelligence ; may see that the moral perceptions of men are perceptions of realities ; and find ground for an abiding faith that this short life does not bound the destiny of the human soul. I then knew the Duke of Argyll, only by his book. I had never been in Scotland, or learned the character as a landlord he bears there. I intended to pay a tribute and give a pleasure to a citizen of the republic of letters, not to irritate a land-owner. I did not think a trumpery title and a patch of ground could fetter a mind that had communed with Nature, and busied itself with causes and beginnings. My mistake was that of ignorance. Since the Duke of Argyll has publicly called attention to it, I thus publicly apologise.

The Duke declares it has not been his aim to argue. This is clear. I wish it were as clear it had not been his aim to misrepresent. He seems to have written for those who have never read the books he criticises. But as those who have done so constitute a very respectable part of the reading world, I can leave his misrepresentations to take care of themselves, confident that the incredible absurdity he attributes to my reasonings will be seen, by whoever reads my books, to belong really to the Duke's distortions. In what I have here to say I prefer to meet him upon his own ground, and to hold to the main question.* I accept the reduction to iniquity.

Strangely enough, the Duke expresses distrust of the very tribunal to which he appeals. " It is a fact," he tells us, " that none of us should ever forget, that the moral faculties do not as certainly revolt against iniquity as the reasoning faculties do against absurdity." If that be the case, why, then, may I ask, is

---

* It is unnecessary for me to say anything of India further than to remark that the essence of " naturalisation " is not in governmental collection of rent, but in its utilisation for the benefit of the people. Nor as to public debts is it worth while to add anything here to what I have said in " Social Problems."

the Duke's whole article addressed to the moral faculties? Why
does he talk about right and wrong, about justice and injustice,
about honour and dishonour, about my "immoral doctrines" and
"profligate conclusions," "the unutterable meanness of the
gigantic villainy" I advocate? Why style me "such a preacher
of unrighteousness as the world has never seen," and so on?
If the Duke will permit me, I will tell him, for in all probability
he does not know—he himself, to paraphrase his own words, being
a good example of how men who sometimes set up as philosophers
and deny laws of the human mind are themselves unconsciously
subject to those very laws. The Duke appeals to moral perceptions for the same reason that impels men, good or bad, learned
or simple, to appeal to moral perceptions whenever they become
warm in argument; and this reason is, the instinctive feeling
that the moral sense *is* higher and truer than the intellectual
sense; that the moral faculties *do* more certainly revolt against
iniquity than the intellectual faculties against absurdity. The
Duke appeals to the moral sense, because he instinctively feels
that with all men its decisions have the highest sanction; and if
he afterwards seeks to weaken its authority, it is because this
very moral sense whispers to him that his case is not a good one.

My opinion as to the relative superiority of the moral and intellectual perceptions is the reverse of that stated by the Duke.
It seems to me certain that the moral faculties constitute a truer
guide than the intellectual faculties, and that what, in reality, we
should never forget, is not that the moral faculties are untrust-
worthy, but that those faculties may be dulled by refusal to heed
them, and distorted by the promptings of selfishness. So true, so
ineradicable is the moral sense, that where selfishness or passion
would outrage it, the intellectual faculties are always called upon
to supply excuse. No unjust war was ever begun without some
pretence of asserting right or redressing wrong, or, despite themselves, of doing some good to the conquered. No petty thief but
makes for himself some justification. It is doubtful if any de-
liberate wrong is ever committed, it is certain no wrongful course
of action is ever continued, without the framing of some theory
which may dull or placate the moral sense.

And while, as to things apprehended solely by the intellectual
faculties, the greatest diversities of perception have obtained and
still obtain among men, and those perceptions constantly change
with the growth of knowledge, there is a striking consensus of

moral perceptions. In all stages of moral development, and under all forms of religion, no matter how distorted by selfish motives and intellectual perversions, truth, justice, and benevolence have ever been esteemed, and all our intellectual progress has given us no higher moral ideals than have obtained among primitive peoples. The very distortions of the moral sense, the apparent differences in the moral standards of different times and peoples, do but show essential unity. Wherever moral perceptions have differed or do differ, the disturbance may be traced to causes which, originating in selfishness and perpetuated by intellectual perversions have distorted or dulled the moral faculty. It seems to me that the Creator, whom both the Duke of Argyll and myself recognise behind physical and mental laws, has not left us to grope our way in darkness, but has, indeed, given us a light by which our steps may be safely guided—a compass by which, in all degrees of intellectual development, the way to the highest good may be surely traced. But just as the compass by which the mariner steers his course over the trackless sea in the blackest night may be disturbed by other attractions, may be misread or clogged, so is it with the moral sense. This evidently is not a world in which men must be either wise or good, but a world in which they may bring about good or evil as they use the faculties given them.

I speak of this because the recognition of the supremacy and certainty of the moral faculties seems to me to throw light upon problems otherwise dark, rather than because it is necessary here, since I admit even more unreservedly than the Duke the competence of the tribunal before which he cites me. I am willing to submit every question of political economy to the tests of ethics. So far as I can see, there is no social law which does not conform to moral law, and no social question which cannot be determined more quickly and certainly by appeal to moral perceptions than by appeal to intellectual perceptions. Nor can there be any dispute between us as to the issue to be joined. He charges me with advocating violation of the moral law in proposing robbery. I agree that robbery is a violation of the moral law, and is therefore, without further inquiry, to be condemned.

As to what constitutes robbery, it is, we will both agree, the taking or withholding from another of that which rightfully belongs to him. That which *rightfully* belongs to him, be it served, not that which legally belongs to him. As to what extent human law may create rights is beside this discussion, for what I propose is to change, not to violate, human law. Such change the Duke declares would be unrighteous. He thus appeals to that moral law which is before and above all human laws, and by which all human laws are to be judged. Let me insist upon this point. Landholders must elect to try their case either by human law or by moral law. If they say that land is rightfully property because made so by human law, they cannot charge those who would change that law with advocating robbery. But if they charge that such change in human law would be robbery, then they must show that land is rightfully property irrespective of human law.

For land is not of that species of things to which the presumption of rightful property attaches. This does attach to things that are properly termed wealth, and that are the produce of labour. Such things in their beginning must have an owner, as they originate in human exertion, and the right of property which attaches to them springs from the manifest natural right of every individual to himself and to the benefit of his own exertions. This is the moral basis of property, which makes certain things rightfully property totally irrespective of human law. The Eighth Commandment does not derive its validity from human enactment. It is written upon the facts of Nature, and self-evident to the perceptions of men. If there were but two men in the world, the fish which either of them took from the sea, the beast which he captured in the chase, the fruit which he gathered, or the hut which he erected, would be his rightful property, which the other could not take from him without violation of the moral law. But how could either of them claim the world as his rightful property? Or if they agreed to divide the world between them, what moral right could their compact give as against the next man who came into the world?

It is needless, however, to insist that property in land rests only on human enactment, which may at any time be changed without violation of moral law. No one seriously asserts any other derivation. It is sometimes said that property in land is derived from appropriation. But those who say this do not really believe it. Appropriation can give no right. The man who raises a cupful of water from the river acquires a right to that cupful, and no one may rightfully snatch it from his hand; but this right is derived from labour, not from appropriation. How could he acquire a right to the river, by merely appropriating it? Columbus did not dream of appropriating the New World to himself and his heirs, and would have been deemed a lunatic had he done so. Nations and princes divided America between them, but by "right of strength." This, and this alone, it is that gives any validity to appropriation. And this, evidently, is what they really mean who talk of the right given by appropriation.

This "right of conquest," this power of the strong, is the only basis of property in land to which the Duke ventures to refer. He does so in asking whether the exclusive right of ownership to the territory of California, which, according to him, I attribute to the existing people of California, does not rest upon conquest, and "if so, may it not be as rightfully acquired by any who are strong enough to seize it?" To this I reply in the affirmative. *If* exclusive ownership is conferred by conquest, then, not merely, as the Duke says, has it "been open to every conquering army and every occupying host in all ages and in all countries of the world to establish a similar ownership," but *it is now open ;* and when the masses of Scotland, who have the power, choose to take from the Duke the estates he now holds, he cannot, if this be the basis of his claims, consistently complain.

But I have never admitted that conquest or any other exertion of force can give right. Nor have I ever asserted, but, on the contrary, have expressly denied, that the present population of California, or any other country, have any exclusive right of ownership in the soil, or can in any way acquire such a right. I hold that the present, the past, or the future population of California, or of any other country, have not, have not had, and cannot have, any right save to the use of the soil, and that as to this their rights are equal. I hold with Thomas Jefferson, "that the earth belongs in usufruct to the living, and that the dead have no power or right over it." I hold that the land was not created for one generation to dispose of, but as a dwelling-place for all generations ; that the men of the present are not bound by any grants of land the men of the past may have made, and cannot grant away the rights of the men of the future. I hold that if all the people of California, or any other country, were to unite in any disposition of the land which ignored the equal right of one of their number, they would be doing a wrong; and that if they could even grant away their own rights, they are powerless to impair the natural rights of their children. And it is for this reason that I hold the titles to the ˉnership of land which the Government of the United States is now granting are of no greater moral validity than the land-titles of the British Isles, which rest historically upon the forcible spoliation of the masses.

How ownership of land was acquired in the past can have no bearing upon the question of how we should treat land now; yet the inquiry is interesting, as showing the nature of the institution. The Duke of Argyll has written a great deal about the rights of landowners, but has never, I think, told us anything of the historical derivation of these rights. He has spoken of his estates, own but has nowhere told us how they came to be his estates. This, I know, is a delicate question, and on that account I will not press it. But while a man ought not to be taunted with the sins of his ancestors, neither ought he to profit by them. And the general fact is, that the exclusive ownership of land has everywhere had its beginning in force and fraud, in selfish greed and unscrupulous cunning. It originated, as all evil institutions originate, in the bad passions of men, not in their perceptions of what is right or their experience of what is wise. "Human laws," the Duke tells us, "are evolved out of human instincts, and, in direct proportion as the accepted ideas on which they rest are really universal, in that same proportion have they a claim to be regarded as really natural, and as the legitimate expression of fundamental truths." If he would thus found on the widespread existence of exclusive property in land an argument for its righteousness, what, may I ask him, will he say to the much stronger argument that might thus be made for the righteousness of polygamy or chattel slavery? But it is a fact, of which I need hardly more than remind him, though less well-informed people may be ignorant of it, that the treatment of land as individual property is comparatively recent, and by at least nine hundred and ninety-nine out of every thousand of those who have lived on this world has never been dreamed of. It is only within the last two centuries that it has, by the abolition of feudal tenures and the suppression of tribal customs, fully obtained among our own people. In fact, even among us it has hardly yet reached full development. For not only are we still spreading over land yet unreduced to individual ownership, but in the fragments of common rights which yet remain in Great Britain, as well as in laws and customs, are there survivals of the older system. The first and universal perception of mankind is that declared by the American Indian chief Black Hawk: "The Great Spirit has told me that land is not to be made property like other

, property. The earth is our mother!" And this primitive perception of the right of all men to the use of the soil from which all must live has never been obscured save by a long course of usurpation and oppression.

But it is needless for me to discuss such questions with the Duke. There is higher ground on which we may meet. He believes in an intelligent Creator; he sees in Nature contrivance and intent; he realises that it is only by conforming his actions to universal law that man can master his conditions and fulfil his destiny.

Let me, then, ask the Duke to look around him in the richest country of the world, where art, science, and the power that comes from the utilisation of physical laws have been carried to the highest point yet attained, and note how few of this population can avail themselves fully of the advantages of civilisation. Among the masses the struggle for existence is so intense that the Duke himself declares it necessary by law to restrain parents from working their children to disease and death! Let him consider the conditions of life involved in such facts as this—conditions, alas! obvious on every side—and then ask himself whether this is in accordance with the intent of Nature.

The Duke of Argyll has explained to me in his "Reign of Law" with what nice adaptations the feathers on a bird's wing are designed to give it the power of flight; he has told me that the claw on the wing of a bat is intended for it to climb by. Will he let me ask him to look in the same way at the human beings around him? I will ask him to consider the little children growing up in city slums, toiling in mines, working in noisome rooms; the young girls chained to machinery all day or walking the streets by night; the women bending over forges in the Black Country or turned into beasts of burden in the Scottish Highlands; the men who all life long must spend life's energies in the effort to maintain life! He should consider them as he has considered the bat and the bird. If the hook of the bat be intended to climb by and the wing of the bird be intended to fly by, with what intent have human creatures been given capabilities of body and mind which under conditions that exist in such countries as Great Britain only a few of them can use and enjoy?

They who see in Nature no evidences of conscious, planning intelligence may think that all this is as it must be; but who that recognises in His works an infinitely wise Creator can for a moment hesitate to infer that the wide difference between obvious intent and actual accomplishment is due, not to the clash of natural laws, but to our ignoring them? Nor need we go far to confirm this inference. The moment we consider in the largest way what kind of an animal man is, we see in the most important of social adjustments a violation of Nature's intent sufficient to account for want and misery and aborted development.

Given a ship sent to sea with abundant provisions for all her company, what must happen if some of that company take possession of the provisions and deny to the rest any share?

Given a world so made and ordered that intelligent beings placed upon it may draw from its substance an abundant supply for all physical needs, must there not be want and misery in such a world if some of those beings make its surface and substance their exclusive property, and deny the right of the others to its use? Here, as on any other world we can conceive of, two and two make four, and when all is taken from anything nothing remains. What we see clearly would happen on any other world does happen on this.

The Duke sees intent in Nature. So do I. That which conforms to this intent is natural, wise, and righteous. That which contravenes it is unnatural, foolish, and iniquitous. In this we agree. Let us then bring to this test the institution which I arraign and he defends.

Place, stripped of clothes, a landowner's baby among a dozen workhouse babies, and who that you call in can tell the one from the others? Is the human law which declares the one born to the possession of a hundred thousand acres of land, while the others have no right to a single square inch, conformable to the intent of Nature or not? Is it, judged by this appeal, natural or unnatural, wise or foolish, righteous or iniquitous? Put the bodies of a duke and a peasant on a dissecting table, and bring, if you can, the surgeon who, by laying bare the brain, or examining the viscera, can tell which is duke and which is peasant. Are not both land animals of the same kind, with like organs and like needs? Is it not evidently the intent of Nature that both shall live on land and use land, in the same way, and to the same degree? Is there not, therefore, a violation of the intent of Nature in human laws which give to one more land than he can possibly use, and deny any land to the other?

Let me ask the Duke to consider, from the point of view of an observer of Nature, a landless man—a being fitted in all his p and powers for the use of land, compelled by all his needs to the use of land, and yet denied all right to land. Is he not as unnatural as a bird without air, a fish without water? And can anything more clearly violate the intent of Nature than the human laws which produce such anomalies?

I call upon the Duke to observe that what Nature teaches us is not merely that men *were* equally intended to live on land, and to use land, and therefore had originally equal rights to land, but that they are *now* equally intended to live on and use land, and, therefore, that present rights to land are equal. It is said that fish deprived of light will, in the course of generations, lose their eyes, and, within certain narrow limits, it is certain that Nature does conform some of her living creatures to conditions imposed by man. In such cases the intent of Nature may be said to have conformed to that of man, or rather to embrace that of man. But there is no such conforming in this case. The intent of Nature, that all human beings should use land, is as clearly seen in children born to-day as it could have been seen in any past generation. How foolish, then, are those who say that although the right to land was originally equal, this equality of right has been lost by the action or sufferance of intermediate generations. How illogical those who declare that, while it would be just to assert this equality of right in the laws of a new country where people are now coming to live, it would be unjust to conform to it the laws of a country where people long have lived! Has Nature anywhere or in anything shown any disposition to conform to what we call vested interests? Does the child born in an old country differ from the child born in a new country?

Moral right and wrong, the Duke must agree with me, are not matters of precedent. The repetition of a wrong may dull the moral sense, but will not make it right. A robbery is no less a robbery the thousand millionth time it is committed than it was the first time. This they forgot who, declaring the slave trade piracy, still legalise the enslavement of those already enslaved. This they forget who, admitting the equality of natural rights to the soil, declare that it would be unjust now to assert them. For as the keeping of a man in slavery is as much a violation of natural right as the seizure of his remote ancestor, so is the robbery involved in the present denial of natural rights to the soil as much a robbery as was the first act of fraud or force which violated those rights. Those who say it would be unjust for the people to resume their natural rights in the land without compensating present holders confound right and wrong as flagrantly as did they who held it a crime in the slave to run away without first paying his owner his market value. They have never formed a clear idea of what property in land means. It means not merely a continuous exclusion of some people from the element which it is plainly the intent of Nature that all should enjoy, but it involves a continuous confiscation of labour and the results of labour. The Duke of Argyll has, we say, a large income drawn from land. But is this income really drawn from land? Were there no men on his land, what income could the Duke get from it, save such as his own hands produced? Precisely as if drawn from slaves, this income represents an appropriation of the earnings of labour. The effect of permitting the Duke to treat the land as his property is to make so many other Scotsmen, in whole or in part, his serfs—to compel them to labour for him without pay, or to enable him to take from them their earnings without return. Surely, if the Duke will look at the matter in this way, he must see that the iniquity is not in abolishing an institution which permits one man to plunder others, but in continuing it. He must see that any claim of landowners to compensation is not a claim to payment for what they have previously taken, but to payment for what they might yet take, precisely as would be the claim of the slaveholder—the true character of which appears in the fact that he would demand more compensation for a strong slave, out of whom he might yet get much work, than for a decrepit one, out of whom he had already forced nearly all the labour he could yield.

In assuming that denial of the justice of property in land is the prelude to an attack upon all rights of property, the Duke ignores the essential distinction between land and things rightfully property. The things which constitute wealth or capital (which is wealth used in production), and to which the right of property justly attaches, are produced by human exertion. Their material is matter, which existed before man, and which man can neither create nor destroy; but their essence—that which gives them the character of wealth—is labour impressed upon or modifying the conditions of matter. Their existence is due to the physical exertion of man, and, like his physical frame, they tend constantly to return again to Nature's reservoirs of matter and for-

Land, on the contrary, is that part of the external universe on which and from which alone man can live; that reservoir of matter and force on which he must draw for all his needs. Its existence is not due to man, but is referable only to that Power from which man himself proceeds. It continues while he comes and goes, and will continue, so far as we can see, after he and his works shall disappear. Both species of things have value, but the value of the one species depends upon the amount of labour required for their production; the value of the other upon the power which its reduction to ownership gives of commanding labour or the results of labour without paying any equivalent. The recognition of the right of property in wealth, or things produced by labour, is thus but a recognition of the right of each human being to himself and to the result of his own exertion; but the recognition of a similar right of property in land is necessarily the impairment and denial of this true right of property.

Turn from principles to facts. Whether as to national strength or national character, whether as to the number of people or as to their physical and moral health, whether as to the production of wealth or as to its equitable distribution, the fruits of the primary injustice involved in making the land, on which and from which a whole people must live, the property of but a portion of their number, are everywhere evil, and nothing but evil.

If this seems to any too strong a statement, it is only because they associate individual ownership of land with permanence of possession and security of improvement. These *are* necessary to the proper use of land, but so far from being dependent upon individual ownership of land they can be secured without it in greater degree than with it. This will be evident upon reflection. That the existing system does not secure permanence of possession and security of improvements in anything like the degree necessary to the best use of land is obvious everywhere, but especially obvious in Great Britain, where the owners of land and the users of land are for the most part distinct persons. In many cases the users of land have no security from year to year—a logical development of individual ownership in land so flagrantly unjust to the user and so manifestly detrimental to the community, that in Ireland, where this system most largely prevailed, it has been deemed necessary for the State to interfere in the most arbitrary ner. In other cases, where land is let for years, the user is often hampered with restrictions that prevent improvement and interfere with use, and at the expiration of the lease he is not merely deprived of his improvements, but is frequently subjected to a blackmail calculated upon the inconvenience and loss which removal would cost him. Wherever I have been in Great Britain, from Land's End to John o' Groat's and from Liverpool to Hull, I have heard of improvements prevented and production curtailed from this cause—in instances which run from the prevention of the building of an outhouse, the painting of a dwelling, the enlargement of a chapel, the widening of a street, or the excavation of a dock, to the shutting up of a mine, the demolition of a village, the tearing up of a railway track, or the turning of land from the support of men to the breeding of wild beasts. I could cite case after case, each typical of a class, but it is unnecessary. How largely use and improvement are restricted and prevented by private ownership of land may be appreciated only by a few, but specific cases are known to all. How insecurity of improvement and possession prevents the proper maintenance of dwellings in the cities, how it hampers the farmer, how it fills the shopkeeper with dread as the expiration of his lease draws nigh, have been, to some extent at least, brought out by recent discussions, and in all these directions propositions are being made for State interference more or less violent, arbitrary, and destructive of the sound principle that men should be left free to manage their own property as they deem best.

Does not all this interference and demand for interference show that private property in land does not produce good results, that it does not give the necessary permanence of possession and security of improvements? Is not an institution that needs such tinkering fundamentally wrong? That property in land must have different treatment from other property, all, or nearly all, are now agreed. Does not this prove that land ought not to be made individual property at all; that to treat it as individual property is to weaken and endanger the true rights of property?

The Duke of Argyll asserts that in the United States we have made land private property because we have found it necessary to secure settlement and improvement. Nothing could be further from the truth. The Duke might as well urge that our protective tariff is proof of the necessity of "protection." We have made land private property because we are but transplanted Europeans, wedded to custom, and have followed it in this matter more readily, because in a new country the evils that at length spring from private property in land are less obvious, while a much larger portion of the people seemingly profit by it—those on the ground gaining at the expense of those who come afterwards. But so far from this treatment of land in the United States having promoted settlement and reclamation, the very reverse is true. What it has promoted is the scattering of population in the country and its undue concentration in cities, to the disadvantage of production and the lessening of comfort. It has forced into the wilderness families for whom there was plenty of room in well-settled neighbourhoods, and raised tenement houses amid vacant lots, led to waste of labour and capital in roads and railways not really needed, locked up natural opportunities that otherwise would have been improved, made tramps and idlers of men who, had they found it in time, would gladly have been at work, and given to our agriculture a character that is rapidly and steadily decreasing the productiveness of the soil.

As to political corruption in the United States, of which I have spoken in "Social Problems," and to which the Duke refers, it springs, as I have shown in that book, not from excess, but from deficiency of democracy, and mainly from our failure to recognise the equality of natural rights as well as of political rights. In comparing the two countries, it may be well to note that the exposure of abuses is quicker and sharper in the United States than in England, and that to some extent abuses which in the one country appear in naked deformity are in the other hidden by the ivy of custom and respectability. But be this as it may, the reforms I propose, instead of adding to corruptive forces, would destroy prolific sources of corruption. Our "protective tariff, our excise taxes, and demoralising system of local taxation would, in their direct and indirect effects, corrupt any government, even if not aided by the corrupting effects of the grabbing for public lands. But the first step I propose would sweep away these corruptive influences, and it is to governments thus reformed, in a state of society in which the reckless struggle for wealth would be lessened by the elimination of the fear of want, that I would give, not the management of land or the direction of enterprise, but the administration of the funds arising from the appropriation of economic rent.

The Duke styles me a pessimist. But, however pessimistic I may be as to present social tendencies, I have a firm faith in human nature. I am convinced that the attainment of pure government is merely a matter of conforming social institutions to moral law. If we do this, there is, to my mind, no reason why in the proper sphere of public administration we should not find men as honest and as faithful as when acting in private capacities.

But to return to the reduction to iniquity. Test the institution of private property in land by its fruits in any country where it exists. Take Scotland. What, there, are its results? That wild beasts have supplanted human beings; that glens which once sent forth their thousand fighting men are now tenanted by a couple of gamekeepers; that there is destitution and degradation that would shame savages; that little children are stunted and starved for want of proper nourishment; that women are compelled to do the work of animals; that young girls who ought to be fitting themselves for wifehood and motherhood are held to monotonous toil in factories; while others, whose fate is sadder still, prowl the streets; that while a few Scotsmen have castles and palaces, more than a third of Scottish families live in one room each, and more than two-thirds in not more than two rooms each; that thousands of acres are kept as playgrounds for strangers, while the masses have not enough of their native soil to grow a flower, are shut out even from moor and mountain, dare not take a trout from a loch or a salmon from a stream!

If the Duke thinks all classes have gained by the advance in civilisation, let him go into the huts of the Highlands. There he may find countrymen of his, men and women the equals in natural ability and in moral character of any peer or peeress in the land, to whom the advance of our wondrous age has brought no gain. He may find them tilling the ground with the crockit spade, cutting grain with the sickle, threshing it with the flail, winnowing it by tossing it in the air, grinding it as their forefathers did a thousand years ago. He may see spinning-wheel and distaff yet in use, and the smoke from the fire in the centre of the hut ascending as it can through the thatch, that the precious heat, which costs so much labour to procure, may be economised to the utmost. These human beings are in natural parts and powers just such human beings as may be met at a royal levee, at a gathering of scientific men or inventors, or captains of industry. That they so live and work is not because of their stupidity, but because of their poverty—the direct and indisputable result of the denial of their natural rights. They have not merely been prevented from participating in the "general advance," but are positively worse off than were their ancestors before commerce had penetrated the Highlands or the modern era of labour-saving inventions had begun. They have been driven from the good land to the poor land. While their rents have been increased, their holdings have been diminished, and their pasturage cut off. Where they once had beasts, they cannot now eat a chicken or keep a donkey, and their women must do work once done by animals. With the same thoughtful attention he has given to "the way of an eagle in the air," let the Duke consider a sight he must have seen many times—a Scottish woman toiling uphill with a load of manure on her back. Then let him apply "the reduction to iniquity."

Let the Duke not be content with feasting his eyes upon those comfortable houses of the large farmers which so excite his admiration. Let him visit the bothies in which farm servants are herded together like cattle, and learn, as he may learn, that the lot of the Scottish farm servant—a lot from which no industry or thrift can release him—is to die in the workhouse, or in the receipt of a parish dole if he be so unfortunate as to outlive his ability to work. Or let him visit those poor broken-down creatures who, enduring everything rather than accept the humiliation of the workhouse, are eking out their last days upon a few shillings from the parish, supplemented by the charity of people nearly as poor as themselves. Let him consider them, and, if he has imagination enough, put himself in their place. Then let him try "the reduction to iniquity."

Let the Duke go to Glasgow, the metropolis of Scotland, where, in underground cellars and miserable rooms, he will find crowded together families who (some of them, lest they might offend the deer) have been driven from their native soil into the great city to compete with each other for employment at any price, to have their children debauched by daily contact with all that is vile. Let him some Saturday evening leave the districts where the richer classes live, wander for a while through the streets tenanted by working people, and note the stunted forms, the pinched features. Vice, drunkenness, the recklessness that comes when hope goes, he will see too. How should not such conditions produce such effects? But he will also see, if he chooses to look, hard, brave, stubborn struggling—the workman who, do his best, cannot find steady employment; the bread-winner stricken with illness; the widow straining to keep her children from the work-house. Let the Duke observe and reflect upon these things, and then apply the reduction to iniquity.

Or let him go to Edinburgh, the modern "Athens," of which Scotsmen speak with pride, and in buildings from whose roofs a bowman might strike the spires of twenty churches he will find human beings living as he would not keep his meanest dog. Let him toil up the stairs of one of these monstrous buildings, let him enter one of those "dark houses," let him close the door, and in the blackness think what life must be in such a place. Then let him try the reduction to iniquity. And if he go to that good charity (but, alas! how futile is Charity without Justice!) where little children are kept while their mothers are at work, and children are fed who would otherwise go hungry, he may see infants whose limbs are shrunken from want of nourishment. Perhaps they may tell him, as they told me, of that little girl, barefooted, ragged, and hungry, who, when they gave her bread, raised her eyes and clasped her hands, and thanked our Father in Heaven for his bounty to her. They who told me that never dreamed, I think, of its terrible meaning. But I ask the Duke of Argyll, did that little child, thankful for that poor dole, get what our Father provided for her? Is He so niggard? If not, what is it, who is it, that stands between such children and our Father's bounty? If it be an institution, is it not our duty to God and to our neighbour to rest not till we destroy it? If it be a man, were it not better for him that a millstone were hanged about his neck and he were cast into the depths of the sea?

There can be no question of over-population—no pretence that Nature has brought more men into being than she has made provision for. Scotland surely is not over-populated. Much land is unused; much land is devoted to lower uses, such as the breeding of game, that might be devoted to higher uses; there are mineral resources untouched; the wealth drawn from the sea is but a small part of what might be drawn. But it is idle to argue this point. Neither in Scotland, nor in any other country, can any excess of population over the power of Nature to provide for them be shown. The poverty so painful in Scotland is manifestly no more due to over-population than the crowding of two-thirds of the families into houses of one or two rooms is due to want of space to build houses upon.

And just as the crowding of people into insufficient lodgings is directly due to institutions which permit men to hold vacant land needed for buildings until they can force a monopoly price from those wishing to build, so is the poverty of the masses due to the fact that they are in like manner shut out from the opportunities Nature has provided for the employment of their labour in the satisfaction of their wants.

Take the island of Skye as illustrating on a small scale the cause of poverty throughout Scotland. The people of Skye are poor—very poor. Is it because there are too many of them? An explanation lies nearer—an explanation which would account for poverty, no matter how small the population. If there were but one man in Skye, and if all that he produced, save enough to give him a bare living, were periodically taken from him and carried off, he would necessarily be poor. That is the condition of the people of Skye. With a population of some seventeen thousand there are, if my memory serves me, twenty-four landowners. The few proprietors who live upon the island, though they do nothing to produce wealth, have fine houses, and live luxuriously, while the greater portion of the rents are carried off to be spent abroad. It is not merely that there is thus a constant drain upon the wealth produced, but that there the power of producing wealth is enormously lessened. As the people are deprived of the power to accumulate capital, production is carried on in the most primitive style, and at the greatest disadvantage.

If there are really too many people in Scotland, why not make the landlords emigrate? They are not merely best fitted to emigrate, but would give the greatest relief. They consume most, waste most, carry off most, while they produce least. As landlords, in fact, they produce nothing. They merely consume and destroy. Economically considered, they have the same effect upon production as bands of robbers or pirate fleets. To national wealth they are as weevils in the grain, as rats in the storehouse, as ferrets in the poultry-yard.

The Duke of Argyll complains of what he calls my "assumption that owners of land are not producers, and that rent does not represent, or represents in a very minor degree, the interest of capital." The Duke will justify his complaint if he will show how the owning of land can produce anything. Failing in this, he must admit that though the same person may be a labourer, capitalist, and landowner, the owner of land, as an owner of land, is not a producer. And surely he knows that the term "rent" as used in political economy, and as I use it in the books he criticises, never represents the interest on capital, but refers alone to the sum paid for the use of the inherent capabilities of the soil.

As illustrating the usefulness of landlords, the Duke says:—

My own experience now extends over the best part of forty years. During that time I have built over fifty homesteads, complete for man and beast. I have drained and reclaimed many hundreds, and inclosed some thousands of acres. In this sense I have added house to house, and field to field, not—as pulpit orators have assumed in similar cases—that I might dwell alone in the land, but that the cultivating class may live more comfortably and with better appliances for increasing the produce of the soil.

And again, he says that during the last four years he has spent on one property £40,000 in the improvement of the soil.

I fear that in Scotland the Duke of Argyll has been "hiding his light under a bushel," for his version of the way in which he has "added house to house and field to field" differs much from that which common Scotsmen give. But this is a matter into which I do not wish to enter. What I would like to ask the Duke is, how he built the fifty homesteads and reclaimed the thousands of acres. Not with his own hands, of course, but with his money. Where, then, did he get that money? Was it not taken as rent from the cultivators of the soil? And might not they, had it been left to them, have devoted it to the building of homesteads and the improvement of the soil as well as he? Suppose the Duke spends on such improvements all he draws in rent, minus what it costs him to live, is not the cost of his living so much waste as far as the improvement of the land is concerned? Would there not be a considerably greater fund to devote to this purpose if the Duke got no rent, and had to work for a living?

But all Scottish-landholders are not even such improvers as the Duke. There are landlords who spend their incomes in racing, in profligacy, in doing things which when not injurious are quite as useless to man or beast as the works of that English Duke, recently dead, who spent vast sums in burrowing underground like a mole. What the Scottish landlords call their "improvements" have, for the most part, consisted in building castles, laying out pleasure-grounds, raising rents, and evicting their kinsmen. But the encouragement given to agriculture, by even such improving owners as the Duke of Argyll, is very much like the encouragement given to traffic by the Duke of Bedford, who keeps two or three old men to open and shut gates he and his have erected across the streets of London. That much the greater part of the incomes drawn by landlords is as completely loss for all productive purposes as though it were thrown into the sea, there can be no doubt. But that even the small part which *is* devoted to reproductive improvement is largely wasted, the Duke of Argyll himself clearly shows in stating, what I have learned from other sources, that the large outlays of the great landholders yield little interest, and, in many cases, no interest at all. Clearly, the stock of wealth would have been much greater had this capital been left in the hands of the cultivators, who, in most cases, suffer from lack of capital, and in many cases have to pay the most usurious interest.

In fact, the plea of the landlords that they, as landlords, assist in production, is very much like the plea of the slaveholders that they gave a living to the slaves. And I am convinced that if the Duke of Argyll will consider the matter as a philosopher rather than as a landlord, he will see the gross inconsistency between the views he expresses as to negro slavery and the position he assumes as to property in land.

In principle the two systems of appropriating the labour of other men are essentially the same. Since it is from land and on land that man must live, if he is to live at all, a human being is as completely enslaved when the land on which he must live is made the property of another, as when his own flesh and blood are made the property of that other. And at least, after a certain point in social development is reached, the slavery that results from depriving men of all legal right to land is, for the very reason that the relation between master and slave is not so direct and obvious, more cruel and more demoralising than that which makes property of their bodies.

And turning to facts, the Duke must see, if he will look, that the effects of the two systems are substantially the same. He is, for instance, an hereditary legislator, with power in making laws which other Scotsmen, who have little or no voice in making laws, must obey under penalty of being fined, imprisoned, or hanged. He has this power, which is essentially that of the master to compel the slave, not because anyone thinks that Nature gives wisdom and patriotism to eldest sons more than to younger sons, or to some families more than to other families, but because as the legal owner of a considerable part of Scotland he is deemed to have greater rights in making laws than other Scotsmen, who can live in their native land only by paying some of the legal owners of Scotland for the privilege.

That power over men arises from ownership of land as well as from ownership of their bodies the Duke may see in varied manifestations if he will look. The power of the Scottish landlords over even the large farmers, and, in the smaller towns, over even the well-to-do shopkeepers and professional men, is enormous. Even where it is the custom to let on lease, and large capital is required, competition, aided in many cases by the law of hypothec, enables the landlord to exert a direct power over even the large farmer. That many substantial farmers have been driven from their homes and ruined because they voted or were supposed to have voted against the wishes of their landlords is well known. A man whose reputation was that of the best farmer in Scotland was driven from his home in this way a few years since for having politically offended his landlord. In Leeds (England) I was told of a Scottish physician who died there lately. He had been in comfortable practice in a village on the estate of a Scottish duke. Because he voted for a Liberal candidate, word was given by the landlord's agent that he was no longer to be employed, and, as the people feared to disobey the hint, he was obliged to leave. He came to Leeds, and, not succeeding in establishing himself, pined away, and would have died in utter destitution but that some friends he had made in Leeds wrote to the candidate for supporting whom he had been boycotted, who came to Leeds, provided for his few days of life, and assumed the care of his children. I mention to his honour the name of that gentleman as it was given to me. It was Sir Sydney Waterlow.

During my recent visit to the Highlands I was over and over again told by well-to-do men that they did not dare to let their opinions be known, or to take any action the landlords or their agents might dislike. In one town such men came to me by night and asked me to speak, but, telling me frankly that they did not dare to apply for a hall, requested me to do that for myself, as I was beyond the tyranny they feared. If this be the condition of the well-to-do, the condition of the crofters can be imagined. One of them said to me, " We have feared the landlord more than we have feared God Almighty; we have feared the factor more than the landlord, and the ground officer more than the factor." But there is a class lower still than even the crofters—the cotters—who, on forty-eight hours' notice, can be turned out of what by courtesy are called their homes, and who are at the mercy of the large farmers or tacksmen, who in turn fear the landlord or agent. Take this class, or the class of farm servants who are kept in bothies. Can the Duke tell me of any American slaves who were lodged and fed as these white slaves are lodged and fed, or who had less of all the comforts and enjoyments of life?

The slaveholders of the South never, in any case that I have heard of, interfered with the religion of the slaves; and the Duke of Argyll will doubtless admit that this is a power which one man ought not to have over another. Yet he must know that at the disruption of the Scottish Church, some forty years ago, Scottish proprietors not merely evicted tenants who joined the Free Church (and in many cases eviction meant ruin and death), but absolutely refused sites for churches, and even permission for the people to stand upon the land and worship God according to the dictates of their conscience. Hugh Miller has told, in the "Cruise of the Betsy," how one minister, denied permission to live on the land, had to make his home on the sea in a small boat. Large congregations had to worship on mountain roadsides without shelter from storm and sleet, and even on the sea-shore, where the tide flowed around their feet as they took the communion. But perhaps the slavishness which has been engendered in Scotland by land monopoly is not better illustrated than in the case where, after keeping them off his land for more than six years, a Scottish duke allowed a congregation the use of a gravel-pit for purposes of worship, whereupon they sent him a resolution of thanks!

In the large cities tyranny of this kind cannot, of course, be exercised, but it is in the large cities that the slavery resulting from the reduction of land to private ownership assumes the darkest shades. Negro slavery had its horrors, but they were not so many or so black as those constantly occurring in such cities. Their own selfish interests, if not their human sympathies or the restraint of public opinion, would have prevented the owners of negro slaves from lodging and feeding and working them as many of the so-called free people in the centres of civilisation are lodged and fed and worked.

With all allowance for the prepossessions of a great landlord, it is difficult to understand how the Duke of Argyll can regard as an animating scene the history of agricultural improvement in Scotland since 1745. From the date mentioned, and the fact that he is a Highlander, I presume that he refers mainly to the Highlands. But as a parallel to calling this history "animating," I can think of nothing so close as the observation of an economist of the Duke's school, who, in an account of a visit to Scotland a generation or so ago, spoke of the pleasure with which, in a workhouse, he had seen "both sexes and all ages, even to infants of two and three years, earning their living by picking oakum," or as the expression of pride with which a Polish noble, in the last century, pointed out to an English visitor some miserable-looking creatures who, he said, were samples of the serfs, any one of whom he could kick as he pleased!

"Thousands and thousands of acres," says the Duke, "have been reclaimed from barren wastes; ignorance has given place to science, and barbarous customs of immemorial strength have been replaced by habits of intelligence and business." This is one side of the picture; but unfortunately there is another side—chieftains taking advantage of the reverential affection of their clansmen, and their ignorance of a foreign language and a foreign law, to reduce those clansmen to a condition of virtual slavery; to rob them of the land which by immemorial custom they had enjoyed; to substitute for the mutual tie that bound chief to vassal and vassal to chief the cold maxims of money-making greed; to drive them from their homes that sheep might have place, or to hand them over to the tender mercies of a great farmer.

"There has been grown," says the Duke, "more corn, more potatoes, more turnips; there has been produced more milk, more butter, more cheese, more beef, more mutton, more pork, more fowls and eggs." But what becomes of them? The Duke must know that the ordinary food of the common people is meal and potatoes; that of these many do not get enough, that many would starve outright if they were not kept alive by charity. Even the wild meat which their fathers took freely, the common people cannot now touch. A Highland poor-law doctor, whose district is on the estate of a prominent member of the Liberal party, was telling me recently of the miserable poverty of the people among whom his official duties lie, and how insufficient and monotonous food was beginning to produce among them diseases like the *pellagra* in Italy, when I asked him if they could not, despite the gamekeepers, take for themselves enough fish and game to vary their diet. "They never think of it," he replied; "they are too cowed. Why, the moment any one of them was even suspected of cultivating a taste for trout or grouse, he would be driven off the estate like a mad dog."

Besides the essays and journals referred to by the Duke of Argyll, there is another publication, which any one wishing to be informed on the subject may read with advantage, though not with pleasure. It is entitled "Highland Clearances," and is published in Inverness by A. McKenzie. There is nothing in savage life more cold-bloodedly atrocious than the warfare here recorded as carried on against the clansmen by those who were their hereditary protectors. The burning of houses; the ejection of old and young; the tearing down of shelters put up to protect women with child and tender infants from the bitter night blast; the threats of similar treatment against all who should give them hospitality; the forcing of poor helpless creatures into emigrant ships which carried them to strange lands and among a people of whose tongues they were utterly ignorant, to die in many cases like rotten sheep, or to be reduced to utter degradation. An animated scene truly! Great districts once peopled with a race, rude it may be and slavish to their chiefs, but still a race of manly virtues, brave, kind, and hospitable—now tenanted only by sheep or cattle, by grouse or deer! No one can read of the atrocities perpetrated upon the Scottish people, during what is called "the improvement of the Highlands," without feeling something like utter contempt for men, who, lions abroad, were such sheep at home that they suffered these outrages without striking a blow, even if an ineffectual one. But the explanation of this reveals a lower depth in the "reduction to iniquity." The reason of the tame submission of the Highland people to outrages which should have nerved the most timid is to be found in the prostitution of their religion. The Highland people are a deeply religious people, and during these evictions their preachers preached to them that their trials were the visitation of the Almighty, and must be submitted to under the penalty of eternal damnation!

I met accidentally in Scotland, recently, a lady of the small landlord class, and the conversation turned upon the poverty of the Highland people. "Yes, they are poor," she said, " but they deserve to be poor; they are so dirty. I have no sympathy with women who won't keep their houses neat and their children tidy."

I suggested that neatness could hardly be expected from women who every day had to trudge for miles with creels of peat and seaweed on their backs.

"Yes," she said, "they have to work hard. But that is not so sad as the hard lives of the horses. Did you ever think of the horses? They have to work all their lives—till they can't work any longer. It makes me sad to think of it. There ought to be big farms where horses should be turned out after they had worked some years, so that they might have time to enjoy themselves before they died."

"But the people?" I interposed. "They, too, have to work till they can't work longer."

"Oh yes!" she replied, "but the people have souls, and even if they have a hard time of it here, they will, if they are good, go to heaven when they die, and be happy hereafter. But the poor beasts have no souls, and if they don't enjoy themselves here they have no chance of enjoying themselves at all. It is too bad!"

The woman was in sober earnest. And I question if she did not fairly represent much that has been taught in Scotland as Christianity. But at last, thank God! the day is breaking, and the blasphemy that has been preached as religion will not be heard much longer. The manifesto of the Scottish Land Restoration League, calling upon the Scottish people to bind themselves together in solemn league and covenant for the extirpation of the sin and shame of landlordism, is a lark's note in the dawn.

As in Scotland so elsewhere. I have spoken particularly of Scotland only, because the Duke does so. But everywhere that our civilisation extends the same primary injustice is bearing the same evil fruit. And everywhere the same spirit is rising, the same truth is beginning to force its way.

HENRY GEORGE.

THE PROPHET OF SAN FRANCISCO.

There are some advantages in being a citizen—even a very humble citizen—in the Republic of Letters. If any man has ever written anything on matters of serious concern, which others have read with interest, he will very soon find himself in contact with curious diversities of mind. Subtle sources of sympathy will open up before him in contrast with sources, not less subtle, of antipathy, and both of them are often interesting and instructive in the highest degree.

A good many years ago a friend of mine, whose opinion I greatly value, was kind enough to tell me of his approval of a little book which I had then lately published. As he was a man of pure taste, and naturally much more inclined to criticism than assent, his approval gave me pleasure. But being a man also very honest and outspoken, he took care to explain that his approval was not unqualified. He liked the whole book except one chapter, "in which," he added, "it seems to me there is a good deal of nonsense."

There was no need to ask him what that chapter was. I knew it very well. It could be none other than a chapter called "Law in Politics," which was devoted to the question how far, in human conduct and affairs, we can trace the Reign of Law in the same sense, or in a sense very closely analogous to that in which we can trace it in the physical sciences. There were several things in that chapter which my friend was not predisposed to like. In the first place he was an active politician, and such men are sure to feel the reasoning to be unnatural and unjust which tends to represent all the activities of their life as more or less the results of circumstances. In the second place, he was above all other things a Free Trader, and the governing idea of that school is that every attempt to interfere by law with anything connected with trade or manufacture is a folly, if not a crime. Now, one main object of my "nonsense" chapter was to show that this doctrine is not true as an absolute proposition. It drew a line between two provinces of legislation, in one of which such interference had indeed been proved to be mischievous, but in the other of which interference had been equally proved to be absolutely required. Protection, it was shown, had been found to be wrong in all attempts to regulate the value or the price of anything. But Protection, it was also shown, had been found to be right and necessary in defending the interests of life, health, and morals. As a matter of historical fact, it was pointed out that during the present century there had been two steady movements on the part of Parliament—one a movement of retreat, the other a movement of advance. Step by step legislation had been abandoned in all endeavours to regulate interests purely economic; whilst, step by step, not less steadily, legislation had been adopted more and more extensively for the regulation of matters in which those higher interests were concerned. Moreover, I had ventured to represent both these movements as equally important—the movement in favour of Protection in one direction being quite as valuable as the movement against Protection in another direction. It was not in the nature of things that my friend should admit this equality, or even any approach to a comparison between the two movements. In promoting one of them he had spent his life, and the truths it represented were to him the subject of passionate conviction. Of the other movement he had been at best only a passive spectator, or had followed its steps with cold and critical toleration. To place them on anything like the same level as steps of advance in the science of government could not but appear to him as a proposition involving "a good deal of nonsense." But critics may themselves be criticised; and sometimes authors are in the happy position of seeing behind both the praise and the blame they get. In this case I am unrepentant. I am firmly convinced that the social and political value of the principle which has led to the repeal of all laws for the regulation of price is not greater than the value of the principle which has led to the enactment of many laws for the regulation of labour. If the Factory Acts and many others of the like kind had not been passed we should for many years have been hearing a hundred "bitter cries" for every one which assails us now, and the social problems which still confront us would have been much more difficult and dangerous than they are.

Certain it is that if the train of thought which led up to this conclusion was distasteful to some minds, it turned out to be eminently attractive to many others. And of this, some years later, I had a curious proof. From the other side of the world, and from a perfect stranger, there came a courteous letter accompanied by the present of a book. The author had read mine, and he sent his own. In spite of prepossessions he had confidence in a candid hearing. The letter was from Mr. Henry George, and the book was " Progress and Poverty." Both were then unknown to fame; nor was it possible for me fully to appreciate the compliment conveyed until I found that the book was directed to prove that almost all the evils of humanity are to be traced to the very existence of landowners, and that by Divine right land could only belong to everybody in general and nobody in particular.

The credit of being open to conviction is a great credit, and even the heaviest drafts upon it cannot well be made the subject of complaint. And so I could not be otherwise than flattered when this appeal in the sphere of politics was followed by another in the sphere of science. Another author was good enough to present me with his book; and I found that it was directed to prove that all the errors of modern physical philosophy arise from the prevalent belief that our planet is a globe. In reality it is flat. Elaborate chapters, and equally elaborate diagrams are devoted to the proof. At first I thought that the argument was a joke, like Archbishop Whately's " Historic Doubts." But I soon saw that the author was quite as earnest as Mr. Henry George. Lately I have seen that both these authors have been addressing public meetings with great success; and considering that all obvious appearances and the language of common life are against the accepted doctrine of Copernicus, it is perhaps not surprising that the popular audiences which have listened to the two reformers have evidently been almost as incompetent to detect the blunders of the one as to see through the logical fallacies of the other. But the Californian philosopher has an immense advantage. Nobody has any personal interest in believing that the world is flat. But many persons may have an interest, very personal indeed, in believing that they have a right to appropriate a share in their neighbour's vineyard.

There are, at least, a few axioms in life on which we are entitled to decline discussion. Even the most sceptical minds have done so. The mind of Voltaire was certainly not disposed to accept without question any of the beliefs that underlay the rotten political system which he saw and hated. He was one of

those who assailed it with every weapon, and who ultimately over-
threw it. Amongst his fellows in that work there was a perfect
revelry of rebellion and of unbelief. In the grotesque procession
of new opinions which have begun to pass across the stage whilst
he was still upon it, this particular opinion against property in
land had been advocated by the famous "Jean Jacques." Voltaire turned his powerful glance upon it, and this is how he treated
it* :—

B. Avez-vous oublié que Jean-Jacques, un des pères de l'Eglise Moderne
a dit, que le premier qui osa clore et cultiver un terrain fut l'ennemi du
genre humain, qu'il fallait l'exterminer, et que les fruits sont à tous, et que
la terre n'est à personne ? N'avons-nous pas déjà examiné ensemble cette
belle proposition si utile à la Société ?

A. Quel est ce Jean-Jacques? Il faut que ce soit quelque Hun, bel
esprit, qui ait écrit cette impertinence abominable, ou quelque mauvais
plaisant, *buffo magro*, qui ait voulu rire de ce que le monde entier a de plus
sérieux. . . .

For my own part, however, I confess that the mocking spirit of
Voltaire is not the spirit in which I am ever tempted to look at the
fallacies of Communism. Apart altogether from the appeal which
was made to me by this author, I have always felt the high
interest which belongs to those fallacies, because of the protean
forms in which they tend to revive and reappear, and because of
the call they make upon us from time to time to examine and
identify the fundamental facts which do really govern the condition of mankind. Never, perhaps, have communistic theories
assumed a form more curious, or lent themselves to more fruitful
processes of analysis, than in the writings of Mr. Henry George.
These writings now include a volume on "Social Problems," published
recently. It represents the same ideas as those which inspire the
work on "Progress and Poverty." They are often expressed in
almost the same words, but they exhibit some development and
applications which are of high interest and importance. In this
paper I shall refer to both, but for the present I can do no more
than group together some of the more prominent features of this
new political philosophy.

In the first place, it is not a little remarkable to find one of the
most extreme doctrines of Communism advocated by a man who
is a citizen of the United States. We have been accustomed to
associate that country with boundless resources, and an almost in-

---

* "Dictionnaire Philosophique," 1764, art. "Loi Naturelle."

exhaustible future. It has been for two centuries, and it still is, the land of refuge and the land of promise to millions of the human race. And among all the states which are there "united," those which occupy the Far West are credited with the largest share in this abundant present, and still more abundant future. Yet it is out of these United States, and out of the one State which, perhaps, above all others, has this fame of opulence, that we have a solitary voice, prophesying a future of intolerable woes. He declares that all the miseries of the Old World are already firmly established in the New. He declares that they are increasing in an ever-accelerating ratio, growing with the growth of the people, and strengthening with its apparent strength. He tells us of crowded cities, of pestilential rooms, of men and women struggling for employments however mean, of the breathlessness of competition, of the extremes of poverty and of wealth—in short, of all the inequalities of condition, of all the pressures and suffocations which accompany the struggle for existence in the oldest and most crowded societies in the world.

I do not pretend to accept this picture as an accurate representation of the truth. At the best it is a picture only of the darkest shadows with a complete omission of the lights. The author is above all things a Pessimist, and he is under obvious temptations to adopt this kind of colouring. He has a theory of his own as to the only remedy for all the evils of humanity; and this remedy he knows to be regarded with aversion both by the intellect and by the conscience of his countrymen. He can only hope for success by trying to convince Society that it is the grasp of some deadly malady. Large allowance must be made for this temptation. Still, after making every allowance, it remains a most remarkable fact that such a picture can be drawn by a citizen of the United States. There can be no doubt whatever that at least as regards many of the great cities of the Union, it is quite as true a picture of them as it would be of the great cities of Europe. And even as regards the population of the States as a whole, other observers have reported on the feverish atmosphere which accompanies its eager pursuit of wealth, and on the strain which is everywhere manifest for the attainment of standards of living and of enjoyment which are never reached except by a very few. So far, at least, we may accept Mr. George's representations as borne out by independent evidence.

But here we encounter another most remarkable circumstance

in Mr. George's books. The man who gives this dark—this almost black—picture of the tendencies of American progress, is the same man who rejects with indignation the doctrine that population does everywhere tend to press in the same way upon the limits of subsistence. This, as is well known, is the general proposition which is historically connected with the name of Malthus, although other writers before him had unconsciously felt and assumed its truth. Since his time it has been almost universally admitted not as a theory but as a fact, and one of the most clearly ascertained of all the facts of economic science. But, like all Communists, Mr. George hates the very name of Malthus. He admits and even exaggerates the fact of pressure as applicable to the people of America. He admits it as applicable to the people of Europe, and of India, and of China. He admits it as a fact as applicable more or less obviously to every existing population of the globe. But he will not allow the fact to be generalised into a law. He will not allow this—because the generalisation suggests a cause which he denies, and shuts out another cause which he asserts. But this is not a legitimate reason for refusing to express phenomena in terms as wide and general as their actual occurrence. Never mind causes until we have clearly ascertained facts; but when these are clearly ascertained let us record them fearlessly in terms as wide as the truth demands. If there is not a single population on the globe which does not exhibit the fact of pressure more or less severe on the limits of their actual subsistence, let us at least recognise this fact in all its breadth and sweep. The diversities of laws and institutions, of habits and of manners, are almost infinite. Yet amidst all these diversities this one fact is universal. Mr. George himself is the latest witness. He sees it to be a fact—a terrible and alarming fact, in his opinion—as applicable to the young and hopeful society of the New World. In a country where there is no monarch, no aristocracy, no ancient families, no entails of land, no standing armies worthy of the name, no pensions, no courtiers, where all are absolutely equal before the law, there, even there—in this paradise of Democracy, Mr. George tells us that the pressure of the masses upon the means of living and enjoyment which are open to them is becoming more and more severe, and that the inequalities of men are becoming as wide and glaring as in the oldest societies of Asia and of Europe.

The contrast between this wonderful confirmation of Malthusian facts, and the vehement denunciation of Malthusian "law," is surely one of the curiosities of literature. But the explanation is clear enough. Mr. George sees that facts common to so many nations must be due to some cause as common as the result. But, on the other hand, it would not suit his theory to admit that this cause can possibly be anything inherent in the constitution of Man, or in the natural System under which he lives. From this region, therefore, he steadily averts his face. There are a good many other facts in human nature and in human conditions that have this common and universal character. There are a number of such facts connected with the mind, another number connected with the body, and still another number connected with the opportunities of men. But all of these Mr. George passes over—in order that he may fix attention upon one solitary fact— namely, that in all nations individual men, and individual communities of men, have hitherto been allowed to acquire bits of land and to deal with them as their own.

The distinction between Natural Law and Positive Institution is indeed a distinction not to be neglected. But it is one of the very deepest subjects in all philosophy, and there are many indications that Mr. George has dipped into its abysmal waters with the very shortest of sounding lines. Human laws are evolved out of human instincts, and these are among the gifts of Nature. Reason may pervert them, and Reason is all the more apt to do so when it begins to spin logical webs out of its own bowels. But it may be safely said that in direct proportion as human laws, and the accepted ideas on which they rest, are really universal, in that same proportion they have a claim to be regarded as really natural, and as the legitimate expression of fundamental truths. Sometimes the very men who set up as reformers against such laws, and denounce as "stupid"* even the greatest nations which have abided by them, are themselves unconsciously subject to the same ideas, and are only working out of them some perverted application.

For here, again, we come upon another wonderful circumstance affecting Mr. George's writings. I have spoken of Mr. George as a citizen of the United States, and also as a citizen of the particular State of California. In this latter capacity, as the citizen

---

* This is the epithet applied by Mr. George to the English people, because they will persist in allowing what all other nations have equally allowed.

of a democratic government, he is a member of that government, which is the government of the whole people. Now, what is the most striking feature about the power claimed by that government, and actually exercised by it every day? It is the power of excluding the whole human race absolutely, except on its own conditions, from a large portion of the earth's surface—a portion so large that it embraces no less than ninety-nine millions of acres, or 156,000 square miles of plain and valley, of mountain and of hill, of lake and river, and of estuaries of the sea. Yet the community which claims and exercises this exclusive ownership over this enormous territory is, as compared with its extent, a mere handful of men. The whole population of the State of California represents only the fractional number of 5·5 to the square mile. It is less than one quarter the population of London. If the whole of it could be collected into one place they would hardly make a black spot in the enormous landscape if it were swept by a telescope. Such is the little company of men which claims to own absolutely and exclusively this enormous territory. Yet it is a member of this community who goes about the world preaching the doctrine, as a doctrine of Divine right, that land is to be as free as the atmosphere, which is the common property of all, and in which no exclusive ownership can be claimed by any. It is true that Mr. George does denounce the conduct of his own Government in the matter of its disposal of land. But strange to say, he does not denounce it because it claims this exclusive ownership. On the contrary, he denounces it because it ever consents to part with it. Not the land only, but the very atmosphere of California—to use his own phraseology—is to be held so absolutely and so exclusively as the property of this community, that it is never to be parted with except on lease and for such annual rent as the government may determine. Who gave this exclusive ownership over this immense territory to this particular community? Was it conquest? And if so, may it not be as rightfully acquired by any who are strong enough to seize it? And if exclusive ownership is conferred by conquest, then has it not been open to every conquering army, and to every occupying host in all ages and in all countries of the world, to establish a similar ownership, and to deal with it as they please?

It is at this point that we catch sight of one aspect of Mr. George's theory in which it is capable of at least a rational explanation. The question how a comparatively small community of men like the first gold-diggers of California and their descendants can with best advantage use or employ its exclusive claims of ownership over so vast an area is clearly quite an open question. It is one thing for any given political society to refuse to divide its vacant territory among individual owners. It is quite another thing for a political society, which for ages has recognised such ownership and encouraged it, to break faith with those who have acquired such ownership, and have lived and laboured, and bought and sold, and willed upon the faith of it. If Mr. George can persaude the State of which he is a citizen, and the Government of which he is in this sense a member, that it would be best never any more to sell any bit of its unoccupied territory to any individual, by all means let him try to do so, and some plausible arguments might be used in favour of such a course. But there is a strong presumption against it and him. The question of the best method of disposing of such territory has been before every one of our great colonies, and before the United States for several generations; and the universal instinct of them all has been that the individual ownership of land is the one great attraction which they can hold out to the settlers whom it is their highest interest to invite and to establish. They know that the land of a country is never so well "nationalised" as when it is committed to the ownership of men whose interest it is to make the most of it. They know that under no other inducement could men be found to clear the soil from stifling forests, or to water it from arid wastes, or to drain it from pestilential swamps, or to enclose it from the access of wild animals, or to defend it from the assaults of savage tribes. Accordingly their verdict has been unanimous; and it has been given under conditions in which they were free from all traditions except those which they carried with them as parts of their own nature, in harmony and correspondence with the nature of things around them. I do not stop to argue this question here; but I do stop to point out that both solutions of it—the one quite as much as the other—involve the exclusive occupation of land by individuals, and the doctrine of absolute ownership vested in particular communities, as against all the rest of mankind. Both are equally incompatible with the fustian which compares the exclusive occupation of land to exclusive occupation of the atmosphere. Supposing that settlers could be found willing to devote the years of labour and of skill which are necessary to make wild soils productive, under no other tenure than that of a long "improvement lease," paying, of course, for some long period either no rent at all, or else a rent which must be purely nominal; supposing this to be true, still equally the whole area of any given region would soon be in the exclusive possession for long periods of time of a certain number of individual farmers, and would not be open to the occupation by the poor of all the world. Thus the absolute ownership which Mr. George declares to be blasphemous against God and Nature, is still asserted on behalf of some mere fraction of the human race, and this absolute ownership is again doled out to the members of this small community, and to them alone, in such shares as it considers to be most remunerative to itself.

And here again, for the third time, we come upon a most remarkable testimony to facts in Mr. George's book, the import and bearing of which he does not apparently perceive. Of course the question whether it is most advantageous to any given society of men to own and cultivate its own lands in severalty or in common is a question largely depending on the conduct and the motives and the character of governments, as compared with the conduct and the character and the motives of individual men. In the disposal and application of wealth, as well as in the acquisition of it, are men more pure and honest when they act in public capacities as members of a Government or a Legislature, than when they act in private capacities towards their fellow-men? Is it not notoriously the reverse? Is it not obvious that men will do, and are constantly seen doing, as politicians, what they would be ashamed to do in private life? And has not this been proved under all the forms which government has taken in the history of political societies? Lastly, I will ask one other question—Is it not true that, to say the very least, this inherent tendency to corruption has received no check from the democratic constitutions of those many "new worlds" in which kings were left behind, and aristocracies have not had time to be established?

These are the very questions which Mr. George answers with no faltering voice; and it is impossible to disregard his evidence. He declared over and over again, in language of virtuous indignation, that government in the United States is everywhere becoming more and more corrupt. Not only are the Legislatures corrupt, but that last refuge of virtue even in the worst societies—the Judiciary

—is corrupt also. In none of the old countries of the world has the very name of politician fallen so low as in the democratic communities of America. Nor would it be true to say that it is the wealthy classes who have corrupted the constituencies. These —at least to a very large extent—are themselves corrupt. Probably there is no sample of the Demos more infected with corruption than the Demos of New York. Its management of the municipal rates is alleged to be a system of scandalous jobbery. Now, the wonderful thing is that of all this Mr. George is thoroughly aware. He sees it, he repeats it in every variety of form. Let us hear a single passage* :—

It behoves us to look facts in the face. The experiment of popular government in the United States is clearly a failure. Not that it is a failure everywhere and in everything. An experiment of this kind does not have to be fully worked out to be proved a failure. But, speaking generally of the whole country, from the Atlantic to the Pacific, and from the Lakes to the Gulf, our government by the people has in large degree become, is in larger degree becoming, government by the strong and unscrupulous.

Again, I say that it is fair to remember that Mr. George is a Pessimist. But whilst remembering this, and making every possible allowance for it, we must not less remember that his evidence does not stand alone. In the United States, from citizens still proud of their country, and out of the United States from representative Americans, I have been told of transactions from personal knowledge which conclusively indicated a condition of things closely corresponding to the indictment of Mr. George. At all events, we cannot be wrong in our conclusion that it is not among the public bodies and Governments of the States of America that we are to look in that country for the best exhibitions of purity or of virtue.

Yet it is to these bodies—legislative, administrative, and judicial, of which he gives us such an account—that Mr. George would confine the rights of absolute ownership in the soil. It is these bodies that he would constitute the sole and universal landlord, and it is to them he would confide the duty of assessing and of spending the rents of everybody all over the area of every State. He tells us that a great revenue, fit for the support of some such great rulers as have been common in the Old World, could be afforded out of one-half the "waste and stealages" of such Municipalities as his own at San Francisco. What would be the "waste and

---

* "Social Problems," p. 22.

stealages" of a governing body having at its disposal the whole agricultural and mining wealth of such States as California and Texas, of Illinois and Colorado?

But this is not all. The testimony which is borne by Mr. George as to what the governing bodies of America now are is as nothing to the testimony of his own writings as to what they would be—if they were ever to adopt his system, and if they were ever to listen to his teaching. Like all Communists, he regards Society not as consisting of individuals whose separate welfare is to be the basis of the welfare of the whole, but as a great abstract Personality, in which all power is to be centred, and to which all separate rights and interests are to be subordinate. If this is to be the doctrine, we might at least have hoped that with such powers committed to Governments, as against the individual, corresponding duties and responsibilities, towards the individual, would have been recognised as an indispensable accompaniment. If, for example, every political society as a whole is an abiding Personality, with a continuity of rights over all its members, we might at least have expected that the continuous obligation of honour and good faith would have been recognised as equally binding on this Personality in all its relations with those who are subject to its rule. But this is not at all Mr. George's view. On the contrary, he preaches systematically not only the high privilege, but the positive duty of repudiation. He is not content with urging that no more bits of unoccupied land should be ever sold, but he insists upon it that the ownership of every bit already sold shall be resumed without compensation to the settler who has bought it, who has spent upon it years of labour, and who from first to last has relied on the security of the State and on the honour of its Government. There is no mere practice of corruption which has ever been alleged against the worst administrative body in any country that can be compared in corruption with the desolating dishonour of this teaching. In olden times, under violent and rapacious rulers, the Prophets of Israel and of Judah used to raise their voices against all forms of wrong and robbery, and they pronounced a special benediction upon him who sweareth to his own hurt and changeth not. But the new Prophet of San Francisco is of a different opinion. Ahab would have been saved all his trouble, and Jezebel would have been saved all her tortuous intrigues if only they could have had beside them the voice of Mr. Henry George. Elijah was a fool. What right could Naboth have to talk about the "inheritance of his fathers"?* His fathers could have no more right to acquire the ownership of those acres on the Hill of Jezreel than he could have to continue in the usurpation of it. No matter what might be his pretended title, no man and no body of men could give it—not Joshua nor the Judges; not Saul nor David; not Solomon in all his glory—could "make sure" to Naboth's fathers that portion of God's earth against the undying claims of the head of the State, and of the representative of the whole people of Israel.

But now another vista of consequence opens up before us. If the doctrine be established that no faith is to be kept with the owners of land, will the same principle not apply to tenancy as well as ownership? If one generation cannot bind the next to recognise a purchase, can one generation bind another to recognise a lease? If the one promise can be broken and ought to be broken, why should the other be admitted to be binding? If the accumulated value arising out of many years, or even generations, of labour, can be and ought to be appropriated, is there any just impediment against seizing that value every year as it comes to be? If this new gospel be indeed gospel, why should not this Californian form of "faith unfaithful" keep us perennially, and for ever "falsely true"?

Nay, more, is there any reason why the doctrine of repudiation should be confined to pledges respecting either the tenancy or the ownership of land? This question naturally arose in the minds of all who read with any intelligence "Progress and Poverty" when it first appeared. But the extent to which its immoral doctrines might be applied was then a matter of inference only, however clear that inference might be. If all owners of land, great and small, might be robbed, and ought to be robbed of that which Society had from time immemorial allowed them and encouraged them to acquire and call their own; if the thousands of men, women, and children who directly and indirectly live on rent, whether in the form of returns to the improver, or of mortgage to the capitalist, or jointure to the widow, or portion to the children, are all equally to be ruined by the confiscation of the fund on which they depend—are there not other funds which would be all swept into the same net of envy and of violence? In particular, what is to become of that great fund on which also thousands and thousands depend—men, women, and children, the

---

* 1 Kings xxi. 3.

aged, the widow, and the orphan—the fund which the State has borrowed and which constitutes the Debt of Nations! Even in "Progress and Poverty" there were dark hints and individual passages which indicated the goal of all its reasoning in this direction. But men's intellects just now are so flabby on these subjects, and they are so fond of shaking their heads when property in land is compared with property in other things, that such suspicions and forebodings as to the issue of Mr. George's arguments would to many have seemed overstrained. Fortunately, in his latter book he has had the courage of his opinions, and the logic of false premises has steeled his moral sense against the iniquity of even the most dishonourable conclusions. All National Debts are as unjust as property in land; all such Debts are to be treated with the sponge. As no faith is due to landowners, or to any who depend on their sources of income, so neither is any faith to be kept with bondholders, or with any who depend on the revenues which have been pledged to them. The Jew who may have lent a million, and the small tradesman who may have lent his little savings to the State—the trust-funds of children and of widows which have been similarly lent—are all equally to be the victims of repudiation. When we remember the enormous amount of the national debts of Europe and of the American States, and the vast number of persons of all kinds and degrees of wealth whose property is invested in these "promises to pay," we can perhaps faintly imagine the ruin which would be caused by the gigantic fraud recommended by Mr. George. Take England alone. About seven hundred and fifty millions is the amount of her Public Debt. This great sum is held by about 181,721 persons, of whom the immense majority—about 111,000—receive dividends amounting to £400 a-year and under. Of these, again, by far the greater part enjoy incomes of less than £100 a-year. And then the same principle is of course applicable to the debt of all public bodies; those of the Municipalities alone which are rapidly increasing, would now amount to something like 150 millions more.

Everything in America is on a gigantic scale, even its forms of villainy, and the villainy advocated by Mr. George is an illustration of this as striking as the Mammoth Caves of Kentucky, or the frauds of the celebrated "Tammany Ring" in New York. The world has never seen such a Preacher of Unrighteousness as Mr. Henry George. For he goes to the roots of things, and shows us how unfounded are the rules of probity, and what mere senseless superstitions are the obligations which have been only too long acknowledged. Let us hear him on National Debts, for it is an excellent specimen of his childish logic, and of his profligate conclusions :—

The institution of public debts, like the institution of private property in land, rests upon the preposterous assumption that one generation may bind another generation. If a man were to come to me and say, "Here is a promissory note which your great-grandfather gave to my great-grandfather, and which you will oblige me by paying," I would laugh at him and tell him that if he wanted to collect his note he had better hunt up the man who made it : that I had nothing to do with my great-grandfather's promises.

And if he were to insist upon payment, and to call my attention to the terms of the bond in which my great-grandfather expressly stipulated with his great-grandfather that I should pay him, I would only laugh the more, and be more certain that he was a lunatic. To such a demand any one of us would reply in effect, "My great-grandfather was evidently a knave or a joker, and your great-grandfather was certainly a fool, which quality you surely have inherited if you expect me to pay you money because my great-grandfather promised that I should do so. He might as well have given your great-grandfather a draft upon Adam, or a cheque upon the First National Bank of the Moon."

Yet upon this assumption that ascendants may bind descendants, that one generation may legislate for another generation, rests the assumed validity of our land titles and public debts.*

Yet even in this wonderful passage we have not touched the bottom of Mr. George's lessons in the philosophy of spoliation. If we may take the property of those who have trusted to our honour, surely it must be still more legitimate to take the property of those who have placed in us no such confidence. If we may fleece the public creditor, it must be at least equally open to us to fleece all those who have invested otherwise their private fortunes. All the other accumulations of industry must be as rightfully liable to confiscation. Whenever "the people" see any large handful in the hands of anyone, they have a right to have it—in order to save themselves from any necessity of submitting to taxation.

Accordingly we find, as usual, that Mr. George has a wonderful honesty in avowing what hitherto the uninstructed world has been agreed upon considering as dishonesty. But this time the avowal comes out under circumstances which are deserving of special notice. We all know that not many years ago the United

---

"Social Problems," pp. 213-14.

States was engaged in a civil war of long duration, at one time apparently of doubtful issue, and on which the national existence hung. I was one of those—not too many in this country—who held from the beginning of that terrible contest that "the North" were right in fighting it. Lord Russell, on a celebrated occasion, said that they were fighting for "dominion." Yes; and for what else have nations ever fought, and by what else than dominion, in one sense or another, have great nations ever come to be? The Demos has no greater right to fight for dominion than Kings; but it has the same. But behind and above the existence of the Union as a nation there was the further question involved whether, in this nineteenth century of the Christian era, there was to be established a great dominion of civilised men which was to have negro slavery as its fundamental doctrine and as the cherished basis of its constitution. On both of these great questions the people of the Northern States—in whatever proportions the one or the other issue might affect individual minds—had before them as noble a cause as any which has ever called men to arms. It is a cause which will be for ever associated in the memory of mankind with one great figure—the figure of Abraham Lincoln, the best and highest representative of the American people in that tremendous crisis. In nothing has the bearing of that people been more admirable than in the patient and willing submission of the masses, as of one man, not only to the desolating sacrifice of life which it entailed, but to the heavy and lasting burden of taxation which was inseparable from it. It is indeed deplorable—nothing I have ever read in all literature has struck me as so deplorable—than that at this time of day, when by patient continuance in well doing the burden has become comparatively light, and there is a near prospect of its final disappearance, one single American citizen should be found who appreciates so little the glory of his country as to express his regret that they did not begin this great contest by an act of stealing. Yet this is the case with Mr. Henry George. In strict pursuance of his dishonest doctrines of repudiation respecting public debts, and knowing that the war could not have been prosecuted without funds, he speaks with absolute bitterness of the folly which led the Government to "shrink" from at once seizing the whole, or all but a mere fraction, of the property of the few individual citizens who had the reputation of being exceptionally rich. If, for example, it were known that any man had made a fortune of

£200,000, the Washington Government ought not to have "shrunk" from taking the whole—except some £200, which remainder might, perhaps, by a great favour, be left for such support as it might afford to the former owner. And so by a number of seizures of this kind, all over the States, the war might possibly have been conducted for the benefit of all at the cost of a very few.*

It may be worth while to illustrate how this would have worked in a single instance. When I was in New York, a few years ago, one of the sights which was pointed out to me was a house of great size and of great beauty both in respect to material and to workmanship. In these respects at least, if not in its architecture, it was equal to any of the palaces which are owned by private citizens in any of the richest capitals of the Old World. It was built wholly of pure white marble, and the owner, not having been satisfied with any of the marbles of America, had gone to the expense of importing Italian marble for the building. This beautiful and costly house was, I was further told, the property of a Scotchman who had emigrated to America with no other fortune and no other capital than his own good brains. He had begun by selling ribbons. By selling cheap, and for ready money, but always also goods of the best quality, he had soon acquired a reputation for dealings which were eminently advantageous to those who bought. But those who bought were the public, and so a larger and larger portion of the public became eager to secure the advantages of this exceptionally moderate and honest dealer. With the industry of his race he had also its thrift, and the constant turning of his capital on an ever-increasing scale, coupled with his own limited expenditure, had soon led to larger and larger savings. These, again, had been judiciously invested in promoting every public undertaking which promised advantage to his adopted country, and which, by fulfilling that promise, could alone become remunerative. And so by a process which, in every step of it, was an eminent service to the community of which he was a member, he became what is called a millionaire. Nor in the spending of his wealth had he done otherwise

---

* Mr. George's words are these : "If when we called on men to die for their country, we had not shrunk from taking, if necessary, nine hundred and ninety-nine thousand dollars from every millionaire, we need not have created any debt."—"Social Problems," p. 216.

than contribute to the taste and splendour of his country, as well as to the lucrative employment of its people. All Nature is full of the love of ornament, and the habitations of creatures, even the lowest in the scale of being, are rich in colouring and in carving of the most exquisite and elaborate decoration. It is only an ignorant and uncultured spirit which denounces the same love of ornament in Man, and it is a stupid doctrine which sees in it nothing but a waste of means. The great merchant of New York had indeed built his house at great cost; but this is only another form of saying that he had spent among the artificers of that city a great sum of money, and had in the same proportion contributed to the only employment by which they live. In every way, therefore, both as regards the getting and the spending of his wealth, this millionaire was an honour and benefactor to his country. This is the man on whom that same country would have been incited by Mr. Henry George to turn the big eyes of brutal envy, and to rob of all his earnings. It is not so much the dishonesty or the violence of such teachings that strikes us most, but its unutterable meanness. That a great nation, having a great cause at stake, and representing in the history of the world a life-and-death struggle against barbarous institutions, ought to have begun its memorable war by plundering a few of its own citizens—this is surely the very lowest depth which has ever been reached by any political philosophy.

And not less instructive than the results of this philosophy are the methods of its reasoning, its methods of illustration, and its way of representing facts. Of these we cannot have a better example than the passage before quoted, in which Mr. Henry George explains the right of nations and the right of individuals to repudiate an hereditary debt. It is well to see that the man who defends the most dishonourable conduct on the part of Governments defends it equally on the part of private persons. The passage is a typical specimen of the kind of stuff of which Mr. George's works are full. The element of plausibility in it is the idea that a man should not be held responsible for promises to which he was not himself a consenting party. This idea is presented by itself, with a careful suppression of the conditions which make it inapplicable to the case in hand. Hereditary debts do not attach to persons except in respect to hereditary possessions. Are these possessions to be kept whilst the corresponding obligations are to be denied? Mr. George is loud on the absurdity of calling upon him to honour any promise which his great-grandfather may have made, but he is silent about giving up any resources which his great-grandfather may have left. Possibly he might get out of this difficulty by avowing that he would allow no property to pass from one generation to another—not even from father to son —that upon every death all the savings of every individual should be confiscated by the State. Such a proposal would not be one whit more violent, or more destructive to society, than other proposals which he does avow. But so far as I have observed, this particular consequence of his reasoning is either not seen, or is kept in the dark. With all his apparent and occasional honesty in confronting results, however anarchical, there is a good deal of evidence that he knows how to conceal his hand. The prominence given in his agitation to an attack on the particular class of capitalists who are owners of land, and the total or comparative silence which he maintains on his desire to rob fundholders of all kinds, and especially the public creditor, is a clear indication of a strategy which is more dexterous than honest. And so it may really be true that he repudiates all hereditary debt because he will also destroy all hereditary succession in savings of any kind. But it must be observed that even thus he cannot escape from the inconsistency I have pointed out, as it affects all public debts. These have all been contracted for the purpose of effecting great national objects, such as the preservation of national independence, or the acquisition of national territory, or the preparations needed for national defence. The State cannot be disinherited of the benefits and possessions thus secured, as individuals may be disinherited of their fathers' gains. In the case of national debts, therefore, it is quite clear that the immorality of Mr. George's argument is as conspicuous as the childishness of its reasoning.

But there are other examples, quite as striking, of the incredible absurdity of his reasoning, which are immediately connected with his dominant idea about property in land. Thus the notion that because all the natural and elementary substances which constitute the raw material of human wealth are substances derived from the ground, therefore all forms of that wealth must ultimately tend to concentration in the hands of those who own the land; this notion must strike a landowner as one worthy only of Bedlam. He may not be able at a moment's notice to unravel all the fallacies on which it rests, and he may even be able to see in it the mad mimicry of logic which deceives the ignorant. But it does not need to be a landowner to see immediately that the conclusion is an absurdity. We have only to apply this notion in detail in order to see more and more clearly its discrepancy with fact. Thus, for example, we may put one application of it thus: All houses are built of materials derived from the soil, of stone, of lime, of brick, or of wood, or of all three combined. But of these materials three are not only products of the soil, but parts of its very substance and material. Clearly it must follow that the whole value of house property must end in passing into the hands of those who own these materials quarries of building-stone, beds of brick earth, beds of lime, and forests. Unfortunately for landowners, this wonderful demonstration does not, somehow, take effect.

But Mr. Henry George's processes in matters of reasoning are not more absurd than his assumptions in matters of fact. The whole tone is based on the assumption that owners of land are not producers, and that rent does not represent, or represents only in a very minor degree, the interest of capital. Even an American ought to know better than this; because, although there are in some parts of the United States immense areas of prairie land which are ready for the plough with almost no preliminary labour, yet even in the New World the areas are still more immense in which the soil can only be made capable of producing human food by the hardest labour, and the most prolonged. But in the old countries of Europe, and especially in our own, every land-owner knows well, and others ought to know a little, that the present condition of the soil is the result of generations of costly improvements, and of renewed and reiterated outlays to keep these improvements in effective order. Yet on this subject I fear that many persons are almost as ignorant as Mr. Henry George. My own experience now extends over a period of the best part of forty years. During that time I have built more than fifty homesteads, complete for man and beast; I have drained and re-claimed many hundreds, and enclosed some thousands, of acres. In this sense I have "added house to house, and field to field," not—as pulpit orators have assumed in similar cases—that I might "dwell alone in the land," but that the cultivating class might live more comfortably, and with better appliances for increasing the produce of the soil. I know no more animating scene than that presented to us in the essays and journals which give an account of the agricultural improvements effected in Scotland since the close of the Civil Wars in 1745. Thousands and thousands of acres have been reclaimed from bog and waste.

Ignorance has given place to science, and barbarous customs of immemorial strength have been replaced by habits of intelligence and of business. In every county the great landowners, and very often the smaller, were the great pioneers in a process which has transformed the whole face of the country. And this process is still in full career. If I mention again my own case, it is because I know it to be only a specimen, and that others have been working on a still larger scale. During the four years since Mr. George did me the honour of sending to me a book assuming that landowners are not producers, I find that I have spent on one property alone the sum of £40,000, entirely on the improvement of the soil. Moreover, I know that this outlay on my own part, and similar outlay on the part of my neighbours, so far from having power to absorb and concentrate in our hands all other forms of wealth, is unable to secure anything like the return which the same capital would have won—and won easily —in many other kinds of enterprise. I am in possession of authentic information that on one great estate in England the outlay on improvements purely agricultural has, for twenty-one years past, been at the rate of £35,000 a-year, whilst including outlay on churches and schools, it has amounted in the last forty years to nearly 2,000,000l sterling. To such outlays landowners are incited very often, and to a great extent, by the mere love of seeing a happier landscape and a more prosperous people. From much of the capital so invested they often seek no return at all, and from very little of it indeed do they ever get a high rate of interest. And yet the whole—every farthing of it—goes directly to the public advantage. Production is increased in full proportion, although the profit on that production is small to the owner. There has been grown more corn, more potatoes, more turnips; there has been produced more milk, more butter, more cheese, more beef, more mutton, more pork, more fowls, and eggs, and all these articles in direct proportion to their abundance have been sold at lower prices to the people. When a man tells me, and argues on steps of logic which he boasts as irrefutable, that in all this, I and others have been serving no interests but our own— nay, more, that we have been but making "the poor poorer" than they were—I know very well that, whether I can unravel his fallacies or not, he is talking the most arrant nonsense, and must have in his composition, however ingenious and however eloquent, a rich combination, and a very large percentage of the fanatic and of the goose.

And here, again, we have a new indication of these elements in one great assumption of fact, and that is the assumption that wealth has been becoming less and less diffused—"the rich richer, the poor poorer." It did not require the recent elaborate and able statistical examination of Mr. Giffen to convince me that this assumption is altogether false. It is impossible for any man to have been a considerable employer of labour during a period embracing one full generation, without his seeing and feeling abundant evidence that all classes have partaken in the progress of the country, and no class more extensively than that which lives by labour. He must know that wages have more than doubled—sometimes a great deal more—whilst the continuous remission of taxes has tended to make, and has actually made, almost every article of subsistence a great deal cheaper than it was thirty years ago. And outside the province of mere muscular labour, amongst all the classes who are concerned in the work of distribution or of manufacture, I have seen around me, and on my own property, the enormous increase of those whose incomes must be comfortable without being large. The houses that are built for their weeks of rest and leisure, the furniture with which these houses are provided, the gardens and shrubberies which are planted for the ornament of them; all of these indications, and a thousand more, tell of increasing comfort far more widely if not universally diffused.

And if personal experience enables me to contradict absolutely one of Mr. George's assumptions, official experience enables me not less certainly to contradict another. Personally I know what private ownership has done for one country. Officially I have had only too good cause to know what State ownership has not done for another country. India is a country in which, theoretically at least, the State is the only and the universal landowner, and over a large part of it the State does actually take to itself a share of the gross produce which fully represents ordinary rent. Yet this is the very country in which the poverty of the masses is so abject that millions live only from hand to mouth, and when there is any—even a partial—failure of the crops, thousands and hundreds of thousands are in danger of actual starvation. The Indian Government is not corrupt—whatever other failings it may have—and the rents of a vast territory can be far more safe if left to its disposal than they could be left at the disposal of such popular governments as those which Mr. George has denounced on the American Continent. Yet somehow the functions and duties which in more civilised countries are discharged by the institution of private ownership in land are not as adequately discharged by the Indian Administration. Moreover, I could not fail to observe, when I was connected with the Government of India, that the portion of that country which has most grown in wealth is precisely that part of it in which the Government has parted with its power of absorbing rent by having agreed to a Permanent Settlement. Many Anglo-Indian statesmen have looked with envious eyes at the wealth which has been developed in Lower Bengal, and have mourned over the policy by which the State has been withheld from taking it into the hands of Government. There are two questions, however, which have always occurred to me when this mourning has been expressed—the first is whether we are quite sure that the wealth of Lower Bengal would ever have arisen if its sources had not been thus protected; and the second is whether even now it is quite certain that any Governments, even the best, spend wealth better for the public interests than those to whom it belongs by the natural processes of acquisition. These questions have never, I think, been adequately considered. But whatever may be the true answer to either of them, there is at least one question on which all English statesmen have been unanimous—and that is, that promises once given by the Government, however long ago, must be absolutely kept. When landed property has been bought and sold and inherited in Bengal for some three generations—since 1793—under the guarantee of the Government that the Rent Tax upon it is to remain at a fixed amount, no public man, so far as I know, has ever suggested that the public faith should be violated. And not only so, but there has been a disposition even to put upon the engagement of the Government an overstrained interpretation, and to claim for the landowners who are protected under it an immunity from all other taxes affecting the same sources of income. As Secretary of State for India I had to deal with this question along with my colleagues in the Indian Council, and the result we arrived at was embodied in a despatch which laid down the principles applicable to the case so clearly that in India it appears to have been accepted as conclusive. The Land Tax was a special impost upon rent. The promise was that this special impost should never be increased; or, in its own words, that there should be no "augmentation of the public assessment in consequence of the improvement of their estates." It was not a promise that no other taxes should ever be raised affecting the same sources of income, provided such taxes were not special, but affected all other sources of income equally. On this interpretation the growing wealth of Bengal accruing under the Permanent Settlement would remain accessible to taxation along with the growing wealth derived from all other kinds of property, but not otherwise. There was to be no confiscation by the State of the increased value of land, any more than of the increased value of other kinds of property, on the pretext that this increase was unearned. On the other hand, the State did not exempt that increased value from any taxation which might be levied also and equally from all the rest of the community. In this way we reconciled and established two great principles which to shortsighted theorists may seem antagonistic. One of these principles is that it is the interest of every community to give equal and absolute security to every one of its members in his pursuit of wealth; the other is, that when the public interests demand a public revenue all forms of wealth should be equally accessible to taxation.

It would have saved us all, both in London and Calcutta, much anxious and careful reasoning if we could only have persuaded ourselves that the Government of 1793 could not possibly bind the Government of 1870. It would have given us a still wider margin if we had been able to believe that no faith can be pledged to landowners, and that we had a Divine right to seize not only all the wealth of the Zemindars of Bengal, but also all the property derived from the same source which had grown up since 1793, and has now become distributed and absorbed among a great number of intermediate shares, standing between the actual cultivator and the representatives of those to whom the promise was originally given. But one doctrine has been tenaciously held by the "stupid English people" in the government of their Eastern Empire, and that is, that our honour is the greatest of our possessions, and that absolute trust in that honour is one of the strongest foundations of our power.

In this paper it has not been my aim to argue. A simple record and exposure of a few of the results arrived at by Mr. Henry George has been all that I intended to accomplish. To see what are the practical consequences of any train of reasoning is so much gained. And there are cases in which this gain is everything. In mathematical reasoning the "reduction to absurdity" is one of the most familiar methods of disproof. In political reasoning the "reduction to iniquity" ought to be of equal value. And if it not found to be so with all minds, this is because of a peculiarity in human character which is the secret of all its corruption, and of the most dreadful forms in which that corruption has been exhibited. In pursuing another investigation I have lately had occasion to observe upon the contrast which, in this respect, exists between our moral and our purely intellectual faculties.* Our Reason is so constituted in respect to certain fundamental truths that those truths are intuitively perceived, and any rejection of them is at once seen to be absurd. But in the far higher sphere of Morals and Religion, it would seem that we have no equally secure moorings to duty and to truth. There is no consequence, however hideous or cruel its application may be, that men have been prevented from accepting because of such hideousness or of such cruelty. Nothing, however shocking, is quite sure to shock them. If it follows from some false belief, or from some fallacious verbal proposition, they will entertain it, and sometimes will even rejoice in it with a savage fanaticism. It is a fact that none of us should ever forget that the moral faculties of Man do not as certainly revolt against iniquity as his reasoning faculties do revolt against absurdity. All history is crowded with illustrations of this distinction, and it is the only explanation of a thousand horrors. There has seldom been such a curious example as the immoral teachings of Mr. Henry George. Here we have a man who probably sincerely thinks he is a Christian, and who sets up as a philosopher, but who is not the least shocked by consequences which abolish the Decalogue and deny the primary obligations both of public and of private honour. This is a very curious phenomenon, and well deserving of some closer investigation. What are the erroneous data—what are the abstract propositions —which so overpower the Moral Sense, and coming from the sphere of Speculation dictate such flagitious recommendations in the sphere of Conduct? To this question I may perhaps return, not with exclusive reference to the writings of one man, but with reference to the writings of many others who have tried to reduce to scientific form the laws which govern the social developments of our race, and who in doing so have forgotten—strangely forgotten—some of the most fundamental facts of Nature.

ARGYLL.

* "Unity of Nature," chap. x., pp. 440-5.

SCOTTISH LAND RESTORATION LEAGUE.

EXECUTIVE, 1884.

OFFICE-BEARERS.

President.

WILLIAM FORSYTH, 32 Buckingham Terrace, Hillhead.

Vice-Presidents.

DEAN OF GUILD BRIMS, Wick.
JAMES M. CHERRIE, Clutha Cottage, Tollcross, Glasgow.
TREASURER COCHRAN, Paisley.
PETER FLEMING, High Street, Dundee.
JAMES HAMILTON, 182 Trongate, Glasgow.
ROBERT HENDRY, 29 Regent Street, Greenock.
D. C. MACDONALD, Solicitor, Aberdeen.
RICHARD M'GHEE, Walthamstow, London.
ALEXANDER M'GUFFIE, 33 Ann Street (City), Glasgow.
T. F. M'KEAN, 10 Pollock Street, Glasgow.
JAMES MACKINTOSH, 87 Argyle, Street, Glasgow.
DAVID M'LARDY, 5 Regent Place, Regent Park, Glasgow.
HUGH MACRAE, Lettermore, Mull.
ROBERT STARKE, 48 West Regent Street, Glasgow.
ANGUS SUTHERLAND, 106 Buccleuch Street, Glasgow.
GEORGE M. SUTHERLAND, Solicitor, Wick.
REV. ALEX. WEBSTER, 8 Belmont Road, Aberdeen.

COMMITTEE.

PETER ANDERSON, 177 Waddell Street, S.S.
FINLAY BELL, 43 Brunswick Street.
WILLIAM BOND, 134 West Graham Street.
PETER BURT, 42 Rosslea Drive.
HUGH CAMPBELL, 182 Trongate Street.
JAMES CLARK, 34 Fisher St., Denniston.
T. W. CRAWFORD, 300 Argyle Street.
WILLIAM EGLIN, 70 York Street.
ROBERT FREELAND, 14 Grafton Street.
J. BRUCE GLASIER, 10 Cavendish St.
ALEX. JAMIESON, 121 Great Hamilton Street.
WILLIAM LOGAN, 27 Ann Street (City).
JOHN MacDONALD, 14 Buchan Street.
EDWARD M'HUGH, 230 Holm Street.
JAMES M'GREGOR, 3 Paul Street.
J. G. MACKAY, 19 Dixon Avenue.
JOHN P. M'LAURIN, 87 Ingram Street.
A. W. MACLEOD, 67 Abbotsford Place.
ALEX. MALCOLM, 34 Ann Street, City.
JAMES MAVER, 134 St Vincent Street.
J. SHAW MAXWELL, 108 Renfield St.
WM. G. MELDRUM, 1 Royal Terrace.
COUNCILLOR D. MORRIN, 153 Parliamentary Road.
JOHN PENMAN, 261 Kennedy Street.
JOHN REID, 6 Anderson St. Partick.
WM. SIMPSON, 145 Queen Street.
JOHN SLAVEN, 109 Castle Street.
JAMES STEVENSON, 16 Main Street, S.S.
JOHN SUTHERLAND, 372 Argyle Street.
REV. WM. L. WALKER, Armadale St., Dennistoun.
HENRY WHYTE, 29 Belgrave Street.
RONALD WRIGHT, Cambuslang.
T. R. YOUNG, 48, Gordon Street.

Hon. Treasurer— JOHN CROSBY, 52 Holmhead Street.

Hon. Secretary—JOHN GOLDIE, 159 Stirling Road.

JOHN MURDOCH, Giffnock, Acting Secretary.

Offices :—80 RENFIELD STREET, GLASGOW.

Open Daily from 10 till 9 p.m.

MANIFESTO.

SCOTTISH LAND RESTORATION LEAGUE.

TO THE PEOPLE OF SCOTLAND.

GREETING,

We, the Committee appointed at a great meeting of the citizens of Glasgow, held in the City Hall, on the evening of 25th February, at which the Scottish Land Restoration League was formed, deem it fitting, in asking the co-operation of our fellow-countrymen, to make a brief statement of our principles and our aims.

We hold that the earth was created by Almighty God as a dwelling-place for the children of men; that it belongs and can belong to no one class or generation, but is a gift fresh from the Creator to each generation whom He calls into being.

We hold that He Who thus gives the earth to the children of men is no respecter of persons, but that, as shown by the facts of Nature no less than by Holy Writ, He has intended all His creatures to be sharers in His bounty, to the end that by their labour, in the manner He has ordained, they may provide for their wants and the wants of those He has made dependent upon them.

We hold that the Equal Right which every man thus derives from his Creator *to the use of the earth* upon which that Creator has called him, is a Right which *no human power* can abrogate or impair; and which exists and must continue to exist despite any or all laws, grants, devices, or bargains which men have made or may make.

We hold that the denial of this First and Most Important of all Human Rights, *the Equal Right to the Possession and Use of the Natural Elements necessary to Life,* is the primary cause of the frightful poverty and misery that, in spite of all our advances in civilisation, exist in our country, and of the vice, crime, and degradation that spring from this poverty.

We hold that the fact that the Land of Scotland—the rightful heritage of the whole people of Scotland—having by a long course of usurpation and fraud been made the private and exclusive property of a few of their number, is the reason why more than two-thirds of Scottish families are compelled to live in houses of one or two rooms; why wages are so pitifully low in every department of industry; and why producers of wealth — those who earn their bread in the sweat of their brow—eat scant and bitter bread, while many of those who do nothing to produce wealth revel in profuse and wanton luxury, drawing from the Scottish people immense sums to be spent in riotous living abroad—the reason why Scotsmen are compelled to emigrate, while great tracts of their native land, from which men have been driven, are given up to beasts and sport.

We hold that those evils which are the result of transgressing and thwarting the declared purpose and benevolent intention of the Creator can be cured only by such a full and complete Restoration of the Land of Scotland to the Scottish People as will secure to the humblest and weakest of our number his *just share* in the land which the Lord our God has given us. To this end we have banded ourselves together, and we hereby call upon the Scottish People everywhere to follow our example and unite with us in a Solemn League and Covenant to spare no effort and no sacrifice to Restore the Soil of Scotland to the People for whom it was intended, and to remove this great shame and crime from the land we love.

This is a question of vital importance to every class in the community; it affects the operative, the miner, the fisherman, the shopkeeper, the merchant, and the professional man as certainly and directly as it does the farmer.

We draw *a clear distinction* between *Property in Land* and *Property in the results of Labour.* The former, we hold, belongs *in usufruct* to the Whole Community; the latter, we hold, belongs rightfully to those who have produced it, or to those to whom the producers have transferred their right. The one we propose to Restore to the Scottish People; the other to leave with those to whom it properly belongs. And although it may be justly held that those who have so long enjoyed the proceeds of the common property should be made not merely to restore it, but to pay proper compensation to those who have been unjustly disinherited, we will not raise this question of compensation, but will be content with the Restoration of the Land to the People.

We propose to effect this Restoration by the simple and obvious expedient of *Shifting all Taxation on to the Value of Land*, irrespective of its use or improvement, and finally *taking all Ground Rent for public purposes*. As a first step to this end we shall demand of our representatives in Parliament a re-imposition of the Tax of FOUR SHILLINGS in the Pound on the Current Value of Land, whether it be rented, or used, or kept idle by its holder; and we shall also demand a measure giving all Towns, Boroughs, and Cities the power to Collect *all* Rates from an Assessment upon the Letting or Rental Value of Land, exclusive of buildings or improvements, and irrespective of use.

These measures can be carried only by such an agitation as will Educate the masses of the People in their Rights and Duties. For this purpose Organisation is necessary; and we therefore call upon all who may be disposed to join with us, to Establish Branches of the Scottish Land Restoration League in all parts of the country.

To carry on the work as it must be carried on funds also will be necessary. These we cannot expect from those animated by the selfish motives which usually induce men to contribute to political funds, and we therefore urge upon those disposed to co-operate with us the necessity of making the Organisation self-supporting.

But while there must be Organisation wherever possible, there is a great field of action, outside of any Organisation, in *personal inquiry* and *private discussion*, in which every one may engage. To this work we earnestly call every Patriot and Lover of Justice, and we would especially urge upon the Ministers of the Gospel of every denomination the importance and religious character of this question—*the Relation between the Soil and the People who live upon it.*

ALEXANDER WEBSTER, CHAIRMAN,
DAVID M'LARDY, SECRETARY,
GLASGOW, *27th February, 1884.*   *For Provisional Committee.*

CONSTITUTION.

I.—TITLE.

THE SCOTTISH LAND RESTORATION LEAGUE.

II.—OBJECT.

Its Object shall be the Restoration of the Land to the People by the abolition of all private property in land, the appropriation of the rent thereof for public purposes, and the relief of the people thereby from all Imperial and local taxation.

III.—MEANS.

The Means employed for the carrying out of the Object of the League shall be the holding of public meetings, the circulation of literature, and such other constitutional means as shall be deemed necessary to create a public sentiment against the evil of Landlordism, and to arouse and organise the people for the purpose of asserting their right to, and recovering possession of, the land.

IV.—MEMBERSHIP.

The Membership of the League shall consist of those who are in sympathy with its object, and who contribute One Shilling Annually.

V.—BRANCHES.

Branches of the League may be formed in any district by any number of persons, not less than ten, who are in sympathy with its object.

Scotland and Scotchmen,

BY

HENRY GEORGE,

AUTHOR OF "PROGRESS AND POVERTY,"

BEING AN ADDRESS DELIVERED IN THE CITY HALL GLASGOW, FEB. 18, 1884.

STARTLING FACTS

ABOUT

PERPETUAL PENSIONS AND LAND TENURE,

Being a Full Report of the Proceedings at the Public Meeting held under the Auspices of the Scottish Land Restoration League, in the City Hall, Glasgow, on Wednesday, 11th June, 1884.

THE RIGHTS OF MAN,

BY HENRY GEORGE,

Author of " Progress and Poverty," " The Land Question : what it involves and how alone it can be settled," etc.

REPRINTED FROM "SOCIAL PROBLEMS."

THE BLIGHT OF LANDLORDISM.

A LETTER

TO THE RIGHT HON. HENRY FAWCETT, M.P.

BY A SCOTTISH LAND RESTORER.

NO COMPENSATION TO LANDLORDS

A NOT UNJUST CONDITION.

By JOHN P. M'LAURIN,

A MEMBER OF THE EXECUTIVE OF THE SCOTTISH LAND RESTORATION LEAGUE.

ONE PENNY EACH.

TO BE HAD OF BOOKSELLERS AND AT

The SCOTTISH LAND RESTORATION LEAGUE.

OFFICE: 80, RENFIELD STREET.

Offices open from 10 a.m. to 9 p.m. for enrollment of members, etc.

Treasurer, JOHN CROSBY ; Secretary, JOHN GOLDIE.

LEAFLET No 2.

FACTS TO THINK ABOUT : Showing the Pressure of the Land Monopoly on the Industrial Classes. 1s. per 100.

CPSIA information can be obtained
at www.ICGtesting.com
Printed in the USA
BVOW06s1418291217
504024BV00007B/47/P